THE HALL OF FAITH SERIES

The Fire That Could Not Die

THE STORY OF THE AZUSA

BY RICK JOYNER

Published & Distributed By
MorningStar Publications
16000 Lancaster Highway
Charlotte, NC 28277-2061

The Fire That Could Not Die

PART 1 • 5
THEY LOVED GOD

PART 2 • 67
GOD WILL DO IT AGAIN

Part 1

They Loved God

CHAPTER ONE

THE ATOMIC AGE OF THE SPIRIT

Over the last two millenniums, the church has experienced many revivals, renewals, and reformation movements. Some have been used to spur the entire church to spiritual advancement. One of the greatest of these was the Azusa Street Revival of 1906 in Los Angeles, California. Nearly one hundred years later, the influence of this revival is not only still felt, but is continuing to increase. The seed of almost every subsequent revival, renewal, or reformation movement can be traced back to this point in the church's history. Just as the pattern for a mature oak tree can be found in the genetic code of an acorn, the pattern for what the church is becoming can be seen in Azusa Street. This is why it is so crucial for us to understand this revival.

Even though such movements are inevitably called "new" when they first appear, they have actually been a progressive restoration of the biblical truth which was lost or neglected during the Middle Ages. At the turn of the century, remnants of the great restoration movements merged, forming a "critical mass." This resulted in gospel explosions that shook the world. The two greatest of these were the revivals in Wales and Los Angeles. Together they ignited powerful changes in the way Christianity has been manifested throughout the world. Having already published a history of the Welsh Revival entitled *The World Aflame*, this booklet is a study of the revival in Los Angeles.

One of the amazing characteristics of this movement is that not only has its impact continued a century after it began, but it is continuing to increase! Through the Pentecostal Revival and the subsequent neo-Pentecostal movements birthed from it (such as the Charismatic, Third Wave, and Apostolic Restoration Movements), there have been more ministers of the gospel ordained, more missionaries sent out, more churches planted, and more people brought to salvation than through any other movement in church history. Studies estimate that nearly 90% of all new converts to Christianity are now coming to Christ through the Pentecostal/Charismatic movements.

To call what began at Azusa Street in Los Angeles just a revival is to obscure its true importance. While it was a revival, Azusa Street was also a renewal movement that resulted in an accelerated reformation of the church. Overall, there may not have been another movement in history that has had a greater impact on the entire church. Its influence has now spanned every denomination and movement to the degree that it would be impossible to understand the present church or her future without understanding this movement.

AN INCREASE IN KNOWLEDGE

The beginning of the 20th century marked the rapid increase of knowledge that the Lord had predicted would come at the end of the age. It has been estimated that it took 5,900 years of man's recorded history for our knowledge of the universe to double. It then doubled again in just decades and is now doubling every few years! As the Apostle Paul wrote in I Corinthians 15:46, **"However, the spiritual is not first, but the natural; then the spiritual."** Running parallel to this great increase of knowledge in the natural has been a similar astonishing recovery of truth in Christianity. The difference is that the Information Age is being fueled by new discoveries, while the great spiritual renewal of the church is being fueled by the rediscovery of the truth that Jesus and His apostles taught.

The Bible itself is more infinite in its scope and depth than anything discovered in the natural world. In recent years, a hidden code was found in the Bible that has astonished the world's greatest scientific minds. The code has such depth and intricacy that it forced even the most vehement secular scientists to declare, "We are not alone!" One stated that the creator of the Bible Code is not only far beyond any human mind, but far beyond even a mind that we can conceive of at this time. Although it took a computer to discover the code, it has been estimated that if every computer in the world were linked together, they still would not have the power to create even the rudiments of this code. The discovery of the Dead Sea Scrolls verifies that the Bible Code was implanted in the Scriptures at least 2,000 years ago, and probably much earlier.

It is interesting that many of the great minds now studying the Bible Code are sure that we are not alone and that there is an intellect in the universe that is beyond our ability to comprehend. They have not yet put the pieces together and concluded that this great intellect is simply the God who wrote the Bible in which the code is found! The fact that God created the code is clearly evident, but they still cannot see Him. However, this, too, reveals an important biblical truth. Even the sharpest human intellect cannot find God unless the Holy Spirit reveals Him.

Parallel to the darkness that keeps even the greatest human genius from seeing God is the Holy Spirit. He is being poured out in such an amazing way that unprecedented multitudes are now coming to a saving knowledge of Jesus Christ. People are now being born again at nearly twice the natural birthrate of the entire world. There is an explosion of both natural and spiritual knowledge, but presently they are on two different tracks, sometimes leading in opposite directions.

Although planted in the Bible by God for a reason, the code is not needed by Christians. The plain text of Scripture itself has limitless intricacies and depths far beyond the capability of a human mind to devise or comprehend without the Holy Spirit. The plain text of the Word of God contains a far higher knowledge than the code, revealing not just what God has done or is doing, but *why*. By studying the plain text of the Bible, we can learn to know the very Person of God. Through His relationships with the men and women recorded in Scripture, we can understand what He expects of us. With this knowledge, we can serve Him, worship Him, and live lives that are pleasing to Him. Our goal must be to not just *know* Him, but also to *obey* Him.

The Word of God is a treasure of unfathomable value. Every "discovery" mined from its pages results in great, sweeping changes in the world. Democracy, free enterprise, and even science have their roots in the discovery, or rediscovery, of biblical truths. The overwhelming majority of the positive influences in civilization can be traced to the Bible. Just as the increase of natural knowledge has brought sweeping changes in the natural realm, there is an increase of spiritual knowledge being released that is bringing great sweeping changes in the church.

The changes coming from the increase of spiritual knowledge are not alterations in the basic truths, morality or integrity upon which Christianity is built. These are ageless and will never change. Nor are the changes an attempt to conform Christianity to modern times. Some of them are, in fact, an expanding and deepening of our biblical and historical moorings. Although the changes are resulting in the expansion of strategies for fulfilling the Great Commission, this also is not their main thrust. The greatest source of this spiritual increase of knowledge is simply a deeper revelation of the person of Jesus Christ: the changes are simply the result of an increasing conformation to His image.

In a very real way, Jesus is Jacob's ladder. He confirmed this when He said to Nathaniel:

"Because I said to you that I saw you under the fig tree, do you believe? You shall see greater things than these."

And He said to him, "Truly, truly, I say to you, you shall see the heavens opened, and the angels of God ascending and descending on the Son of Man" (John 1:50-51).

The Lord was making a direct reference to the ladder that Jacob had seen, as recorded in Genesis 28:12-13:

And he [Jacob] had a dream, and behold, a ladder was set on the earth with its top reaching to heaven; and behold, the angels of God were ascending and descending on it.

And behold, the LORD stood above it and said, "I am the LORD, the God of your father Abraham and the God of Isaac; the land on which you lie, I will give it to you and to your descendants."

Jesus is Jacob's ladder in the sense that earthly messengers of God's Word ascend into the heavenly places by a progressive revelation of Him. As we behold more of His glory, we are changed more into His image. The result of true knowledge is not some esoteric understanding of spiritual things, but is rather our transformation into the nature of Christ. Knowing Him is how we ascend into the heavenly places to sit with Him and is also how we are enabled to descend to the world to represent Him.

The great revivals now taking place around the earth are all the result of an increasing receptivity to the Holy Spirit, Who leads us in an increasing devotion to a personal relationship with Jesus Christ. Such a great, worldwide receptivity to the Holy Spirit by the church largely began with the Azusa Street Revival of 1906.

CHANGE IS ACCELERATING

The Scriptures are clear that the Lord is going to return for a bride without spot or wrinkle (Ephesians 5:27). She will be pure, holy, unified, and so powerful that the nations will tremble at her presence. Many look at the outward conditions of the church and think that either this is impossible or it would take a thousand years to accomplish. However, as Peter asserted in II Peter 3:8, **"But do not let this one fact escape your notice, beloved, that with the Lord one day is as a thousand years, and a thousand years as one day."** The Lord can do in one day what we think would take a thousand years. God can speed things up, and He is doing so.

In the natural and spiritual realms, change is accelerating. Those who resist change are breaking and being discarded like old wineskins. Movements, denominations, and churches that stop moving are now dying quickly. Those who have learned to ride the wave of the Holy Spirit are growing at a rate that was unthinkable just a few years ago. In the midst of this greatly increasing pace of change, there are traditions and historic moorings that can help us to more safely navigate, but we must not let them become anchors that stop our progress. The cloud of God's presence is moving forward at a very fast pace.

For mostly economic purposes, the world has devised efficient means to process and use new discoveries. In general, the church has not done as well, and many of the great truths that should have been the domain of the church have been stolen by the world and put to less than noble use. We are not experiencing changes simply for the sake of change, but because the church is headed for her destiny. We must define both where we are going and why. As the parable of the talents exhorts, we must manage wisely the great treasures of knowledge entrusted to us so that their maximum benefit is obtained (Matthew 25:14-30).

Even so, all that is going on spiritually today is far beyond any human ability to control. The Lord Jesus is the Head of His church, and He is the only One who can manage His own household. However, Jesus does delegate responsibilities. There is a desperate need for all who are called to leadership to have deep roots and clear vision if we are to stay close to Him through this incredible time of change, properly managing what has been appointed to us. This requires understanding.

It is not enough for us to just "take more spiritual land." We must be able to hold onto what is gained. As Proverbs 24:3-4 states, **"By wisdom a house is built, and by understanding it is established; and by knowledge the rooms are filled with all precious and pleasant riches."**

Great increase of knowledge can fill our houses, but we must first have the wisdom to build and the understanding to establish them. Our goal must be more than just having large churches; it must be to have a house in which God wants to dwell. Our goal must be to see a church without spot or wrinkle, a glorious bride prepared for the coming of her King. What good is the most glorious temple if the Lord is not in it?

Just a few centuries ago, great battles were fought over the right of individual Christians to be free to read their own Bibles. Thousands upon thousands died in these wars, even though very few people were literate and could have read a Bible if there had been the freedom to do so. What was accomplished through their efforts was for our sake. Regardless of what we attain in our time, we are standing on the shoulders of all who went before us, fighting and taking the land whose fruit we are now eating.

Today, most Christians have several Bibles. We are bombarded with spiritual knowledge and revelations of truth to the degree that not even the largest mega church could absorb them all, much less apply them. But this is all right. No one church is called to possess and apply *all* spiritual knowledge and revelation. Each church has a role to play, and we need to stay focused on our part. Even so, it does help for us to have at least a concept of the "big picture," or where the entire church is headed.

We must also honor our "fathers" and "mothers" so that our days may be long upon the earth (Exodus 20:12). Many great revivals and spiritual movements die prematurely because they neglect this matter. This principle is so crucial to the Lord that it was the only commandment He gave with a promise attached, which was longevity. To obey this commandment, we must acknowledge that our progress is largely due to the faith and courage of our spiritual fathers and mothers. Heritage is important, which is why the Lord instructed every generation of Israel to celebrate certain feasts in remembrance of what God had done in previous generations.

We must remember, though, that the Lord was not just called **"the God of**

Abraham," but also **"the God of Abraham, the God of Isaac, and the God of Jacob" (Exodus 3:6),** meaning that He wants to relate to every generation. Therefore, we are studying the Azusa Street Revival, not only to gain greater understanding and to honor our spiritual forefathers, but also to have our hearts stirred in such a way that we, too, will yearn for our own encounters with the Lord. We cannot be content to just recount the stories, but we must earnestly desire to see God move again. Just as Frank Bartleman said that he would rather die than not see revival, we must have a like passion to see God move in our own lives.

UNDERSTANDING THE PAST

God *is* moving. We are well into the spiritual atomic age. As previously stated, the pace of spiritual change has already exceeded our ability to understand and implement all that is happening. However, the release of different movements, the interchange among them, and the timing of the release of rediscovered truths, combined with the conditions in the world, make it clear that the Holy Spirit is very much in control. An understanding of the essence of past spiritual movements is essential for anyone who is called to leadership in these times if we are going to be responsive to what the Spirit is doing.

Of course, there are many individuals, churches, and even whole denominations that were birthed out of the Azusa Street Revival that have stopped growing. In many places, one can only find the remnants of the past glory, with little or no continuing fire. However, around the world there are multitudes of Pentecostal/Charismatic churches that are ablaze with the presence and activity of God. In countries where the greatest advances of the gospel are now taking place, Pentecostal and Charismatic Christians are at the vanguard.

Like most other movements, the Pentecostal Movement had a spectacular beginning, followed by upheaval from within and persecution from without. Many mistakes were made that threatened to sidetrack the entire movement. These were almost always resolved in a way that resulted in greater stability to the movement, enabling it to continue advancing. The lessons learned from these situations will help any advancing church or movement.

Understanding the mistakes made by others can help us to avoid the same traps.

However, before we become too concerned with how to avoid the traps of revival, we need to know how to start one! Because the most important step in any journey is the first, understanding how true moves of God begin is crucial: this is the essence of our study. We will look at some mistakes, but we should be far more concerned with what was done right. To take a few hours to examine our history can save us years of being sidetracked in the future.

In all that we study, we must recognize that the seed of the church is Jesus Christ. We can look at Him and know whom we are to resemble. When we examine Scripture, the church, or history, He is the One for whom are looking. It is reported that after Michelangelo finished his great sculpture of King David, he was asked how he did it. He replied that he had a picture of King David in his heart and cut away all of the stone that wasn't him. In a sense, this is what those who are called to be "master builders" in the church must do. We must have a clear picture of Jesus in our hearts and remove everything that is not Him. That is likewise what we will seek to do with this important history.

CHAPTER TWO

THE SEED

The strength and longevity of anything that is built will be affected by the strength of the foundation upon which it is built. The church that is built upon the foundation of Jesus Christ will prevail just as He did. Any other foundation will ultimately fail. We must not even build upon the foundation of the Holy Spirit. He was sent to lead us to Jesus Christ, and in all that we do we must be seeking Him.

The Apostle Paul also warned that we must be careful how we build upon the foundation. He declared that all **"wood, hay [and] stubble"** will be burned up, and that only the gold, silver and precious stones will remain (I Corinthians 3:12- 15 KJV). Therefore, in our studies of churches or movements, we should look for things that have proven to be **"wood, hay [and] stubble,"** which do not last, as well as for those things which have proven to be gold, silver and precious stones, which do last.

The beginning of the Pentecostal Movement is usually marked from the outpouring of the Holy Spirit at Azusa Street in 1906.

There were a number of powerful ministries and movements which both experienced and promulgated the baptism of the Holy Spirit prior to Azusa Street, but none of them had the continuing impact of this revival. It was a true beginning, adding something to the advancing church that has lasted. The movement has changed and now has many different streams, but one can recognize what originated at Azusa Street as the source for most of the moves of God that have established the course of Christianity in this century.

William J. Seymour and Frank Bartleman are the two names most often associated with the Azusa Street Revival. They were different in many ways, but they were both young men who had an uncommon desire to know the Lord and see His power restored to the church. Seymour was the unquestioned leader of the revival. He had the authority that gave birth to the movement on earth. Bartleman was the intercessor who had authority in heaven.

Because these men were so different, their stories give us two very different views of the Azusa Street Revival. However, these different pictures do not conflict, but rather compliment one another to give us a more complete picture. As Seymour was the actual leader of the Azusa Street Revival, we will begin with his story. But first we must go back a little further in history.

THE GRANDFATHER OF THE REVIVAL

Charles Fox Parham (1873-1929) presided over a Bible school in Topeka, Kansas. He was a true spiritual father, and many consider him the father of the modern Pentecostal Movement. Even though he would later reject many of his own spiritual children, his part in this movement must be recognized and understood.

Parham was a seeker of God who was constantly challenged by what he viewed as the great chasm between biblical Christianity and the state of the church in his day. He sought the Lord for what he considered to be the true, biblical expression of Christianity. As he was keeping a prayer vigil on New Year's Eve of the year 1900, he experienced the spiritual gift of "speaking in tongues," or "glossolalia" in the early hours of January 1, 1901, the beginning of the 20th century. Few could have understood how this one event would be used to define Christianity in the 20th century.

Speaking in tongues, or the use of other spiritual gifts, was by no means unique in church history. Many reformers and revivalists had such experiences. Even so, Parham's experience came at what could be called the "fulness of time," a time that was ripe for the harvest of a recovered truth. His experience created a great deal of interest, at least in part due to the dry and lifeless state of the church in his day. Also, Parham was not known for emotionalism or exaggeration. Rather, he was conservative and resolute, which at the time gave even more credibility to his experience.

A couple of years after his experience, Parham became ill and was forced to move to Houston where he could stay with friends. When his strength recovered, he began another Bible school in the Texas port city. William Seymour became one of his students, but because he was black and Parham was a strict segregationist, Seymour had to sit outside of the classroom and listen through a door that Parham would leave cracked open for him.

Seymour wanted the Lord so much that he would embrace any humiliation to be close to what the Lord was doing. He was convinced that a new Pentecost was coming to the church and that what Parham had experienced at the dawning of the century was a prophetic indication of what was to come.

REJECTION

William J. Seymour was born in Centerville, Louisiana on May 2, 1870. He was the son of former slaves, Simon and Phyllis Seymour. Even after gaining their freedom, the Seymours continued working on a plantation. Growing strong in body and spirit, young William followed in their footsteps, but received little formal education. He taught himself to read so that he could read the Bible. Under the constant harassment of the Ku Klux Klan and the oppressive Jim Crow laws, William became convinced that Jesus Christ was the only true liberator of men. After contracting small pox and losing one eye, he devoted himself to the ministry, proclaiming the gospel of the true liberty of all men and women through Jesus Christ.

Without having received the baptism in the Holy Spirit that he had sought for so long, Seymour left Parham's school in January of 1906 to pastor a mission congregation. Just a week after his arrival, he was rejected by congregational leaders of the mission who did not like his emphasis on the coming of a new Pentecost. Seymour started a little prayer group of like-minded souls who simply had to experience more of God. They had no clue that when they found what they were looking for, the Christian world would be changed forever.

One recurring theme in church history seems to be that great leaders often arrive at their appointed place of destiny because of rejection. We see this repeated in Scripture in the accounts of the lives of Joseph, Moses, David, and the Lord Jesus Himself, to name but a few. It seems as if great disappointment with ourselves or others is a prerequisite for being used by God in a great way, especially to begin something new. It could even be said that learning to deal with rejection comes on the list of instructions for being a Christian. We should never be surprised by rejection, but must keep our trust and attention on the Lord. He will use everything that happens to us for His own good, as well as for ours.

Long before Seymour made his way to Los Angeles, Frank Bartleman had been preparing the spiritual ground for what was coming. He was not a pastor, but a layman who loved the Lord and loved his city.

Longing to see the Lord move in Los Angeles, he prayed continuously for God to intervene.

A Growing Expectation

On April 8, 1904, Frank Bartleman heard F.B. Meyer preach. Meyer was from London, and he described the revival then going on in Wales. Meyer had met Evan Roberts, the leader of the Welsh Revival, and was greatly impacted by him. Meyer was not a starter of revival fires, but he was a carrier of the flame. His descriptions of the revival in Wales would throw fuel on the flames of the flickering spiritual fires of all who heard him. After listening to Meyer, Frank Bartleman promised the Lord that He would have his full devotion from that time on. Many make such commitments in the heat of the moment, but Bartleman was a man of his word, and he kept his promise.

With his heart broken from the recent death of his three-year-old daughter, Bartleman felt that his treasure was now in heaven, and he resolved to do everything for the sake of the gospel. He began distributing tracts at the post office, banks, public buildings, saloons and even houses of prostitution. Working long and faithfully but seeing few lives changed, Bartleman yearned for more power.

A great burden came upon him to see the kind of revival that he had heard about in Wales, which not only changed individuals, but changed whole cities. The more he worked, the more he travailed in heart for such a move of God to come to Los Angeles. Then Bartleman began to sense that what was to come to Los Angeles would be different from what was happening in Wales, and he began to boldly prophesy the coming of "another Pentecost."

At this time, many other Christians around the world, seemingly independent of one another, were growing in an expectation of this gift of the Holy Spirit being poured out on the church again as He had in the first century. This was due to an emphasis on the biblical prophecies in both Joel 2 and Acts 2 which promised that this would happen in the last days. In this way, the ground was tilled for the rapid spreading of this movement when the Holy Spirit would come. In God's perfect timing, some of these people would come together in the little, run-down mission on Azusa Street.

This is one of the unique elements of the Azusa Street Revival—it was not just centered around one person. Just as Barnabas had to find Paul before he could be released into his own calling as an apostle, our own destinies are often dependent on our humility to seek out those to whom we need to be joined in order to accomplish His purposes. Even Jesus submitted Himself to the ministry of John the Baptist before proceeding with His own calling. The Lord has so composed His plan that we all need one another. The more we humble ourselves to be joined to others, the more fruit we will ultimately bear.

On the first of May, a small revival broke out in the Lake Avenue Methodist Episcopal Church in Pasadena. Intercessors had been praying for a revival in Pasadena, and the Lord answered their prayers. Bartleman visited the church and was deeply touched. The altar area full of seeking souls encouraged his resolve to see the Lord move in the same way in Los Angeles.

That night he made a prophetic notation in his journal. He began listing the future dangers that would surely try to sidetrack the coming great revival, which he was already convinced was near. He wrote that it would pass many churches by because they were satisfied, and that ultimate success or failure would depend on people staying humble enough to seek the grace of God. Bartleman believed that if those who were used in the revival became caught up with a sense of their own importance, this great spiritual opportunity would be lost. He wrote:

God has always sought a humble people. He can use no other...There is always much need for heart preparation, in humility and separation, before God can consistently come. The depth of any revival will be determined exactly by the spirit of repentance that is obtained. In fact, this is the key to every true revival born of God.

Bartleman then read the book, *The Great Revival in Wales,* by S.B. Shaw, and the fire in his heart could no longer be contained. He forsook his secular employment and devoted himself full time to the ministry. He was at the point where he would either see revival or perish. He hungered so much for it that he even lost his appetite for food. "Man shall not live by bread alone," he declared to those who were concerned for him. In his heart, he had determined that it would be better to die than to miss the opportunity to see a great move of God. Bartleman had so abandoned himself to God that he simply did not have any alternatives. He had nothing to fall back on in his life if God did not move. Since Jesus called His first disciples, such has been the nature of the pillars upon whom the Lord has built His church.

Bartleman began visiting with people daily, giving them G. Campbell Morgan's pamphlet entitled the "Revival in Wales." Morgan's writing deeply moved the hearts of many, and some were enlisted to pray for a mighty outpouring of the Holy Spirit in Los Angeles. Bartleman became so consumed with God that he began to awaken in the middle of the night shouting praises to Him. He wrote of this time:

I was now going day and night, exhorting myself to have faith in God for mighty things. The spirit of revival consumed me. The spirit of prophecy came upon me strongly also. I seemed to receive a definite "gift of faith" for revival. We were evidently in the beginning of wonderful days to come, and I prophesied continually of a mighty outpouring.

Bartleman's zeal for the Lord at this time was so great that his wife and friends began to fear for his life. He missed so much sleep and so many meals in order to pray that they did not think he could last much longer. His response to their pleas for moderation was that he would rather die than not see revival.

Psalm 104:4 states that the Lord makes His messengers **"flames of fire."** This was the impartation that the Lord gave to the two men on the Road to Emmaus—hearts that burned for the message of the Son of God. Bartleman was such a messenger. The fire that burned within him could not be quenched. Because of this, Bartleman would be used to start revival fires around the world.

CHAPTER THREE

THE HEAT BUILDS

On June 17, Bartleman went to Los Angeles to attend a meeting at the First Baptist Church where they were waiting on God for an outpouring of the Spirit. Their pastor, Joseph Smale, had just returned from Wales. He was filled with zeal to receive the same visitation and blessing of the Holy Spirit in his own church which was now holding meetings every day and night.

Visiting this church often, Bartleman became discouraged by the fact that the people waited on the pastor before doing anything. They would not even pray until he came. This stirred Bartleman to seek a deeper revelation of Jesus for himself. He would sleep fitfully, often awakening to pray and seek the Lord for a closer relationship with Him. The closer he grew to the Lord, the harder it was on his flesh, but he did not care. He wanted to know **"the fellowship of His sufferings" (Philippians 3:10)** and the travail that the Lord felt for the lost. He began to experience what he later felt were the **"groanings too deep for words" (Romans 8:26).**

At a tent meeting, Bartleman met Edward Boehmer, who had just been converted the previous spring and shared the same burden of prayer. Immediately, they were united in spirit and seemed to feed one another's fire for revival. Bartleman later said, "My life was by this time literally swallowed up in prayer. I was praying day and night."

It was at this time that a concern arose in Bartleman for what he perceived to be an overemphasis on the Welsh Revival. It was news of that great revival that had first stirred his own heart, but he became uncomfortable with everyone praying for a revival like the one in Wales. He sensed that God wanted to do something different in Los Angeles.

Bartleman then wrote a letter to Evan Roberts in Wales asking him to pray for California. Roberts replied that he would, and this gave the church in Los Angeles her first link to the Welsh Revival leaders. Roberts exhorted them: "Congregate the people together who are willing to make a total surrender. Pray and wait. Believe God's promises. Hold daily meetings." This letter was a great encouragement to Bartleman. The Spirit was surely moving throughout the city. Conviction was rapidly spreading among the people, and they were rallying from all over Los Angeles to meet at Pastor Smale's church.

Because of Bartleman's exhortations, the people were gradually allowing the Spirit to conduct the meetings and not just looking to Pastor Smale, which was, in fact, the model of the Welsh Revival. Souls were saved as meetings progressed, unguided by human hands.

The Holy Spirit always requires that the people be in unity before He moves in a great way. Just as the disciples had gathered **"all with one accord" (Acts 2:1 KJV)** on the day of Pentecost when the Holy Spirit was first poured out, unity was coming to many in Los Angeles. As sectarian barriers were swept away, there was a sense of the nearness of the match that was about to set the kindling on fire.

REPENTANCE IS THE KEY

By this time, meetings were not just running day and night, but often through the night. Spreading through the people was an almost uncontrollable passion for the Lord. Pastor Smale began to prophesy of wonderful things to come, including "the speedy return of the apostolic gifts to the church." People began to feel as if Los Angeles was a type of Jerusalem where the

Spirit first came to dwell in men and women. By June of 1905, the prayers had changed from praying for another revival like the one in Wales to praying for "another Pentecost."

On July 3, Bartleman and Boehmer were in a hall in Pasadena praying when the burden became almost unbearable for them, and they cried out like women giving birth. When the burden finally lifted, they just sat for awhile, enjoying the calm that enveloped them. Suddenly the Lord Jesus revealed Himself, standing between them. They did not dare to move. Love swept over them and they felt as if a burning fire went through them. As Bartleman later wrote,

My whole being seemed to flow down before Him, like wax before the fire. I lost all consciousness of time or space, being conscious only of His wonderful presence. I worshiped at His feet. It seemed a veritable Mount of Transfiguration. I was lost in the pure Spirit. The Lord had said nothing to us, but only overwhelmed our spirits by His presence. He had come to strengthen and assure us for His service. We knew now we were workers with Him, fellowshippers of His sufferings, in the ministry of "soul travail." Real soul travail is just as definite in the spirit as natural human birth-pangs.

The simile is almost perfect in its sameness.
No soul is ever born without this. All true
revivals of salvation come this way.

It was at this time that Bartleman was
reminded of what he felt was the keynote to
revival: "The depth of revival will be determined exactly by the depth of the spirit of
repentance. And this will hold true for all
people, at all times."

The revival spirit at Pastor Smale's church
was rapidly spreading over the city. Devoted
intercessors came from all over the region,
representing almost all spiritual back-
grounds. Soon they expanded their vision
from just seeing a revival in California to
praying for the nation. Then they took
another step of faith and began praying for
a revival that would touch the ends of the
earth. As Bartleman wrote, "The spirit of
prophecy began to work among us for
mighty things on a large scale."

While visiting Smale's church again,
Bartleman was led to pray for faith, discernment of spirits, healing, and prophecy.
When a few believers had begun praying for
revival a few months before, no one seemed
to have much faith for anything out of the
ordinary. There was a scepticism regarding
the present conditions of the church that

cast itself like a pall over believers. With consistent intercession, this attitude changed. Now they had faith to not only pray for great things, but to prophesy them.

It was then that Bartleman wrote an article for the *Daily News of Pasadena* describing what he saw in Pastor Smale's church. When it was printed, the publisher was inspired to come and see what was going on. Greatly convicted, he came to the altar and sought God earnestly. He then wrote his own article entitled, "What I Saw in a Los Angeles Church" that was copied in a number of holiness papers throughout the country. This created a nationwide interest in what was happening in Los Angeles.

After the meetings had run daily in the First Baptist Church for almost four months, the officials of the church were tired and wanted to return to the old order. Pastor Smale was told either to stop the revival or to get out. He chose the latter and organized a New Testament Church. Although he had expressed his dislike for such organizations, Bartleman became a charter member. He preached daily wherever he could find an audience and prayed continuously in between.

CHAPTER FOUR

THE DARK NIGHT OF THE SOUL

After several months at such an intense level, many began to faint and drift away. The spiritual heat that was building began to ebb. It was like the children of Israel leaving Egypt with such zeal, only to have it wither away quickly in the wilderness they were required to cross before arriving in the Promised Land. The same thing occurred just before the outbreak of the Welsh Revival. The same thing also had happened before the day of Pentecost when the Spirit was first given to the church. More than 500 had seen the resurrected Christ and were instructed to wait for the gift of the Holy Spirit in Jerusalem, but only 120 were left when He was poured out on those gathered.

During this time, Bartleman's zeal did not wane. The burden for intercession so possessed him that he fasted and prayed continually. Fearing that he could not survive much longer, his wife and friends tried desperately to persuade him to stop pushing himself so intensely. Bartleman later said that he felt as if he were at Gethsemane with the Lord. He began to think that the travail of the Lord's soul had fallen upon him in such measure that he would not live to see the answer to his prayers. Still, he continued.

Some believed that Bartleman was losing his mind. Few could understand what he was going through. This was the apostolic intercession that compelled Paul to risk his life in **"stripes, in imprisonments, in tumults, in labours, in watchings, in fastings" (II Corinthians 6:5 KJV).** He submitted to beatings, stonings, or anything else required for the sake of the gospel. To the **"natural man,"** such sacrifices are foolish because they are the **"things of the Spirit" (I Corinthians 2:14)** which selfish people cannot understand. Bartleman held onto his faith, believing that **"he who has found his life shall lose it" (Matthew 10:39). "Except a corn of wheat fall into the ground and die, it abideth alone: but *if it die*, it bringeth forth much fruit" (John 12:24 KJV).** He did not care if he had to die; he needed revival more than he needed life.

The New Testament Church started by Brother Smale grew and began to take on so many secondary interests that the people began to lose interest in prayer. As they drifted away from carrying the burden for revival, Bartleman likewise drifted away from them. Many start strongly, but do not endure long. However, even if he alone was left, Frank Bartleman was determined to pray until the fire of God fell.

TWO BY TWO

As Bartleman continued his unyielding zeal for revival and prayer, opposition to him arose in the church. Some tried to influence him to stop his prayer meetings. When Bartleman inquired of the Lord for His will, he had an encounter with the glory of the Lord. Without answering his questions directly, the Lord settled the matter. Bartleman was addicted to the presence of God and would rather do without air than prayer. **"'We ought to obey God rather than men'"** he quoted when asked what he was going to do (Acts 5:29).

It was at this time that Bartleman wrote another article that fanned the sparks back into flames for many who had drifted from their hope for revival. In it, he concluded with a prophecy that was soon to be fulfilled:

Heroes will arise from the dust of obscure and despised circumstances, whose names will be emblazoned on heaven's eternal page of fame. The Spirit is brooding over our land again as at creation's dawn, and the decree

*of God goes forth— "Let there be light!"
Brother, sister, if we all believed God, can
you realize what would happen? Many of us
here are living for nothing else. A volume of
believing prayer is ascending to the throne
night and day. Los Angeles, Southern California, and the whole continent shall surely
find itself before long in the throes of a mighty
revival, by the Spirit and power of God (Way
of Faith, November 16, 1905).*

After a service in the New Testament
Church, Bartleman and a few others were
led to pray for the Lord to pour out His
Spirit speedily, with signs following (Mark
16:17). They did not have "tongues" in
mind, and later asserted that at the time
they had not even heard or thought of such
a thing. This was in February of 1906.

On March 26, Bartleman went to a
cottage meeting on Bonnie Brae Street.
Both white and black believers were meeting there for prayer. He had just met
William Seymour, who had come from
Texas. Of that meeting he recorded in his
journal a simple note about Seymour: "He
was a black man, blind in one eye, very plain,
spiritual, and humble. He attended the
meetings at Bonnie Brae Street."

When Bartleman met Seymour, it marked the beginning of the dawn after his dark night of the soul. Both men lived and breathed passion for revival. It is unlikely that they ever sat down to discuss how they would work together, but it is obvious that the Azusa Street Revival would not have been possible without either one of them. One was nitro and the other was glycerin. Alone, they each were not accomplishing much, together they created an explosion that rocked the entire Christian world. The Lord still sends His disciples out two by two. Regardless of who we are and what the Lord has entrusted to us, we will not be able to accomplish what we have been called to do without others. Like the meeting of Paul and Barnabas, the meeting of Seymour and Bartleman stands as one of the great demarcations in the history of Christianity.

CHAPTER FIVE

THE FIRE FALLS AT AZUSA

Seymour had recognized the hand of God in his rejection by the mission and was content serving the little home prayer group which met regularly for several months. Seymour's hope was not in the appearance of things on the earth, but in what God would send out of heaven. While in the middle of a ten-day fast, Seymour and the others in this little band were dramatically baptized in the Holy Spirit and received the gift of tongues, as well as other charismatic gifts.

As previously noted, this outpouring of the Holy Spirit was not unique in history, but never before had this experience itself become an actual movement. This time it did. Word spread "like fire in a dry wood," and like the first Pentecost, multitudes came to see what had happened at Seymour's prayer group. This was caused by Frank Bartleman's stream of articles, tracts and faithful ministry throughout the city, exhorting churches and prayer groups to seek the Lord for "a new Pentecost."

As soon as word went out about the experience of Seymour's prayer group, large crowds of interested people descended on them. To accommodate the hungry people, the prayer group was forced to rent an old, rundown, barn-like building in the middle of a black ghetto. At the time, no one imagined that the little street on which it was located would soon become one of the most famous addresses in the world.

The former mission was once used as a livery stable and had a dirt floor. Many remarked when they visited Azusa Street that the Lord, Himself, had been born in such a place. The rent was only $8.00 a month, and the building could hold as many as 900 people. Even so, services were soon continuing almost around the clock to handle the crowds.

Meanwhile, the little group at Bonnie Brae had been tarrying earnestly for an outpouring of the Holy Spirit and on April 9, the Spirit had come to them in a manner similar to the way He had come on the original Day of Pentecost. On Sunday morning, April 15, a black sister from the Bonnie Brae meeting attended the service at New Testament Church and spoke in tongues, creating a great stir. Similar to the first Pentecost, people gathered in little groups on the sidewalk after the service, inquiring what this might mean.

What had begun as a spark with Charles Parham now leapt into open flames, eventually capturing the attention of millions around the world, and quickly spreading to every recognized nation on earth. A humble little prayer group, led by a one-eyed, former sharecropper, was the seed bed for the dawning of a new age in Christianity. When Bartleman heard of it that Sunday morning, he went to Bonnie Brae immediately. He later wrote of that day:

We had been praying for many months for victory. Jesus was now "showing Himself alive" again to many. The pioneers had broken through for the multitude to follow.

There was a general spirit of humility manifested in the meeting. They were taken up with God. Evidently the Lord had found the little company at last, outside as always, through whom He could have His way. God had not chosen an established mission where this could be done. They were in the hands of men; the Spirit could not work. Others far more pretentious had failed. That which man esteems had been passed by once more, and the Spirit born again in a humble "stable" outside ecclesiastical establishments.

A body must be prepared, in repentance and humility, for every outpouring of the Spirit. The preaching of the Reformation was begun by Martin Luther in a tumble down building in the midst of the public square in Wittenberg. D'Aubigne describes it as follows:

In the middle of the square at Wittenberg stood an ancient wooden chapel, thirty feet long and twenty feet wide, whose walls, propped up on all sides, were falling into ruin. An old pulpit made of planks, and three feet high, received the preacher. It was in this wretched place that the preaching of the Reformation began. It was God's will that which was to restore His glory should have the humblest surroundings. It was in this wretched enclosure that God willed, so to speak, that His well-beloved Son should be born a second time. Among those thousands of cathedrals and parish churches with which the world is filled, there was not one at that time which God chose for the glorious preaching of eternal life.

Like most of the great moves of God in history, when the great Pentecostal revival began, very few understood the true significance of what was happening, including those who had been used to prophesy its coming. It did not start as a large mass movement, but as a little prayer meeting.

This is a part of the wonder and awe of being a Christian.

When we are relating to Almighty God, the One who created the world with a word, anything upon which He decides to breathe can have consequences far beyond any human comprehension. Since He is God, He can take the most humble prayer meeting and use it to shake the world. Because He delights in using the humble, the weak, and the foolish, a simple meeting can have historic consequences. We must never doubt the potential of even the most humble gathering of those who know Him. If just two can agree together, anything is possible. Whenever two or more gather, He will be there (Matthew 18:19-20).

BREAKING THE NORM

The Lord usually does great things after a time of preparation. He uses men and women who, like Frank Bartleman, have such a passion for the Lord and His purposes that they impart it to others. When the fire is finally lit, it can then jump all human imposed boundaries and move beyond human control.

Every great spiritual pioneer who has been used to ignite great moves of God initially has seemed reckless and dangerous to the church they are sent to awaken. Seymour and Bartleman were no exceptions to this. They wanted God so much that they did not care what anyone else thought about them. They could not live within the present limits of their times, so they were used to push those limitations back. Their abandonment to the Spirit was then used to benefit the multiplied millions who would follow.

From the beginning, the Azusa Street Revival was astonishingly unique, breaking many norms. Even the first meetings contained the seeds of the great movements that would be birthed from it. The following is Bartleman's own description of his first visits to the little mission on Azusa Street:

After a season of prayer, I was impressed of the Lord to go to the meeting which had been removed from Bonnie Brae Street to 312 Azusa Street. Here they had rented an old frame building, formerly a Methodist church, in the center of the city but now a long time out of use for meetings. It had become a receptacle for old lumber, plaster, etc. They had cleared space enough in the surrounding dirt and debris to lay some planks on top of empty nail kegs, with seats enough for possibly thirty people. If I remember rightly, these were arranged in a square facing one another.

I was under tremendous pressure to get to the meeting that evening. It was my first visit to Azusa Mission. Mother Wheaton, who was living with us, was going with me. She was so slow that I could hardly wait for her. We finally reached Azusa and found about a dozen saints there, some white, some black. Brother Seymour was in charge. The "Ark of God" moved off slowly, but surely, at Azusa. It was carried on the shoulders of His own appointed priests in the beginning. We had no "new cart" in those days to please the carnal, mixed multitude. We had the devil to fight, but the Ark was not drawn by oxen (dumb beasts). The priests were "alive unto God," through much preparation and prayer.

Discernment was not perfect, and the enemy got some advantage which brought reproach to the work, but the saints soon learned to "take the precious from the vile." The combined forces of hell were set determinedly against us in the beginning. It was not all blessing. In fact, the fight was terrific. As always, the devil combed the country for crooked spirits to destroy the work if possible. But the fire could not be smothered. Gradually the tide arose in victory. But from a small beginning, a very little flame.

It was soon noised abroad that God was working at Azusa, and all kinds of people began to come to the meetings. Many were curious and unbelieving, but others were hungry for God. The newspapers began to ridicule and abuse the meetings, thus giving us much free advertising. This brought the crowds. The devil overdid himself again. Outside persecution never hurt the work. We had the most to fear from the working of evil spirits within. Even spiritualists and hypnotists came to investigate, and to try their influence. Then all the religious sore heads, crooks and cranks came, seeking a place in the work. We had the most to fear from these. But this is always the danger to every new work; they had no place elsewhere. This condition cast a fear over many which was hard to overcome. It hindered the Spirit much. Many were afraid to seek God for fear the devil might get them.

We found early in the Azusa work that when we attempted to steady the Ark, the Lord stopped working. We dared not call the attention of the people too much to the working of the evil one. Fear would follow. We could only pray and then God would give us victory. There was a presence of God with us, through prayer, we could depend on. The *leaders had limited experience, and the wonder is that the work survived at all against its powerful adversaries. But it was of God. That was the secret.*

A certain writer has well said, "On the day of Pentecost, Christianity faced the world, a new religion without a college, a people, or a patron. All that was ancient and venerable rose up before her in solid opposition, and she did not flatter or conciliate any one of them. She assailed every existing system and every bad habit, burning her way through innumerable forms of opposition. This she accomplished with her 'tongue of fire' alone."

Another writer has said, "The apostasy of the early Church came as a result of a greater desire to see the spread of its power and rule than to see new natures given to its individual members. The moment we covet a large following and rejoice in the crowd that is attracted by our presentation of what we consider truth, and have not a greater desire to see the natures of individuals changed according to the divine plan, we start to travel the same road of apostasy..."

"TO THE ENDS OF THE EARTH"

The leaders of the Azusa work were inexperienced in leadership, but well-seasoned in faith. They trusted Him to make up their lack, and for as long as they maintained their humility, He did. It survived every onslaught of the devil and the religiously deceived. Missionaries and Christian leaders came from the far corners of the earth, and God touched all who came as sincere seekers of His grace.

One of the great spiritual pioneers of the 20th century, Dr. A.G. Garr, closed his ministry at the Burning Bush Hall to go to Azusa. He received his baptism in the Holy Spirit and quickly departed, going first to India and then to China to spread the fire, making him the first modern Pentecostal missionary. Through Dr. Garr, hundreds of missionaries in the field received the baptism. Within a year, the fires of Pentecost were burning around the world. Dr. Garr would also pioneer the use of tents for revivals and skits for street outreaches, eventually producing the first Christian television program. He emphasized the Lord's love for healing to the degree that for the entire time that he pastored in Charlotte, North Carolina, no one in his congregation needed a doctor.

Brother Smale came to Azusa to look up his members, many of whom had left to be a part of the new move of God. He invited them back, promising them liberty in the Spirit. Many returned and for a time the Lord moved mightily at the New Testament Church also.

A. S. Worrell, translator of the New Testament, visited Azusa and declared that the work there had "rediscovered the blood of Christ for the Church at that time." Great emphasis was placed on the blood of Christ, and a high standard for "a clean life" was raised from the very beginning. When presumptuous men would try to use the meetings for their own platform, strange things would happen to them. Some would lose their breath so that they could not speak. Others would forget what they wanted to say and sit down. Some even seemed temporarily blinded. According to Bartleman, no one got away with presumption in the early meetings.

Just as it was written of the first-century church, it was often said of the revival at Azusa that the people experienced continual awe and wonder at the great things that God was doing. Every day was set on fire by the acts of God.

CHAPTER SIX

MAKING DISCIPLES OF ALL NATIONS

A remarkable characteristic of the Azusa Street Revival from the beginning was the diversity of the people who were drawn to it. Some likened it to the Day of Pentecost when men and women from every nation had gathered in Jerusalem. Even a prominent Jewish rabbi in Los Angeles announced his full support of the revival. Soon, remarkable healings and dramatic conversions were taking place almost daily. The church at the time was so dry that each testimony went forth like sparks into dry wood. Newspaper articles fanned the sparks into flames. Testimonies from the Welsh Revival had stirred thousands to seek the Lord for revival in America, and the deplorable spiritual state of the country made her ready for it. Because of these conditions, the fire spread faster than possibly any previous or subsequent revival in American history.

Seymour started a little paper to teach about the renewal and answer questions. He printed 5,000 copies which were passed around until they fell apart. Although he soon was printing 50,000, Seymour was unable to keep up with the demand.

Within weeks, a steady stream of missionaries was coming from every continent on earth. Those who were on the front lines of the battle against the forces of darkness were the most acutely aware that they needed more power. Just as the Lord told His disciples that they would receive power to be His witnesses when the Holy Spirit came upon them, this same baptism had become the only hope for effective ministry. They came as desperate seekers and left filled with the power they had sought. Within months, gospel fires were burning all over the world. In just two years, the movement had taken root in more than 50 nations and was thought to have penetrated every U.S. town with a population of more than 3,000.

Because missionaries were some of the first to come to Azusa Street, missions remain a fundamental part of the spiritual genetic code of the Pentecostal Movement and one of its greatest strengths. Throughout Scripture, God has demonstrated His greatest power where there was the greatest darkness. The first ones to carry the Pentecostal movement abroad were seasoned missionaries who used the power they had been given. Multitudes of men, women and children were delivered from bondage with the help of these newly empowered missionaries. Those who were delivered went forth to deliver others. Soon missionary reports sent back to home churches read like a modern-day book of Acts, adding even more fuel to the fire of the movement.

CHILDREN BECOME FATHERS

The Apostle Paul lamented that there were many teachers but not many fathers (I Corinthians 4:15). A spiritual father does more than just teach: he reproduces in others what he has received. There was an essence to the Pentecostal Revival from the beginning that compelled everyone not to merely learn *about* the Lord, but to *know* Him through personal experience. When it was learned that the greatest demonstrations of the Spirit's power usually came in the darkest, neediest places, many were compelled to go on mission trips just to witness the power of God. This added great strength and depth to the new movement, awakening the entire church to the needs of the nations and inspiring her to ignite the fire throughout the world.

Pentecostal children grew up continually hearing from missionaries the testimonies of God's power. Because such esteem was given to them, missionaries often became the children's greatest heroes. Emulating these courageous men and women, many of the children of the early Pentecostal pioneers grew up to be missionaries so that they could be close to the wonderful activities of the Spirit. Others became pastors and evangelists who founded new churches and ministries all around the world. Many of them are now leaders of Pentecostal churches and denominations, each one a vast treasure house filled with stories of the glory of God.

These men and women of God walked with Him, learning His ways and how to be hosts of His Holy Spirit. They grew up believing that the book of Acts was not just a history book, but a living guide for normal church life, and many of their own stories read like a modern-day book of Acts as they earned their place as elders of the church.

We do not see in order to believe, but we believe in order to see. Because it is basic Pentecostal theology that God is the same today as He was yesterday, and that He does everything today that He did in Scripture, true Pentecostals believe and witness His present-day work. Many Pentecostals will begin to wonder where they have gone wrong if they are not witnessing regular demonstrations of the power of God. To them it is blasphemy to think that God was an author who wrote just one book and then retired. They must have a living relationship with a living God, and so they do see His great works.

This was the experience at Azusa Street. Believers were in constant awe at the works of God in their midst. People would not eat or sleep—sometimes for days at a time—because they were so caught up in the presence of the Lord. Like the manna that came from heaven, each day they expected a fresh experience with the Lord. Faith built on faith until the humble little mission really had become a window of heaven.

At any given time, the Azusa Street Mission would be packed with such a diversity of people that some considered this almost as much of a marvel as the extraordinary miracles that were taking place. Although the revival began with a few black men and women in a little home group, soon most of those who came were white. In one meeting, more than 20 nationalities were counted. Fine ladies could be found lying prostrate on the floor next to domestic servants and washer women. Prominent churchmen and high government officials sat next to hobos. No one seemed to care. They all had one thing in common—they came to receive the Holy Spirit of God.

When we see through the Lord's eyes, we will not know each other after the flesh, but after the Spirit. The more that we are able to see with the eyes of the Spirit, the closer we will come to the Lord's ultimate purpose for His church—to be a house of prayer for all nations.

CHAPTER SEVEN

DEFEATED BY A SECONDARY SUCCESS

It seems that the Lord had ordained Pastor Smale to be the one to ignite the great Pentecostal outpouring of the 20th century. While Smale could have had this honor for eternity, he relinquished it because he fell over the same stumbling block that has tripped countless others. His local congregation became so successful that he lost his bigger vision. As Harry Truman once said, "We are often defeated by our secondary successes."

This is not to belittle in any way the importance of building our churches. Local congregations are the front line of what God is doing in the earth, and they need to be the primary focus of the overwhelming majority of Christian leaders. However, when one is called to a larger purpose as Smale was called, good can be the worst enemy of best. Where would the church today be if Paul had rejected the apostolic call so that he could stay to build up the local church at Antioch? While we possibly would be in the same place because God could have used someone else, it is likely that we never would have heard of Paul.

Smale became a respected pastor of a nice little church, but he could have been used to spark one of God's greatest moves of all time. That honor now belongs to William J. Seymour, a humble black man who loved God more than any human honors or earthly riches. Seymour began the movement that shook the world and redefined modern Christianity. In heaven, Seymour is certainly named with the great reformers of the church.

Gracious in his analysis of what transpired when Smale rejected the call to go on, Bartleman said: "God found His Moses in the person of Brother Smale to lead us to the Jordan crossing. But He chose Brother Seymour for our Joshua, to lead us over."

Bartleman stayed with the mission for a long time before he received the baptism in the Holy Spirit. After his baptism, he had an encounter with the Lord that would direct him for the rest of his life. The following is his own description of this encounter:

After God filled me, His Spirit rested mightily upon me one morning, and He said to me: "If you were only small enough, I could do anything with you." A great desire to be little, yea, to be nothing, came into my heart. But it has been oh so hard to keep low enough

*for Him to really work through me. And He
only really uses me when I am little in my
own eyes and really humble at His feet.*

*The fact is, when a man gets to the place
where he really loves obscurity, where he does
not care to preach, and where he would
rather sit in the back seat than on the
platform, then God can lift him up and use
him, and not very much before.*

This seemed to be a summation of a
primary message from God through Azusa.
As long as the people are willing to be
obscure and not jockey for position or
recognition, the fire not only continues to
burn, but increases. As soon as self-seeking,
or self-preservation enters, the end is near.
This is precisely what brought an end to the
role that the little mission on Azusa Street
played in what was to become one of the
greatest moves of God in history. Seymour
was used mightily to begin the revival and
lead it through its most fragile times, but
then he, too, succumbed to the temptation
to exalt the lesser purposes above the
higher one.

For many months, the little mission was
filled with the glory of God. Awe and wonder
at the great things that God was doing
permeated every meeting. The larger and

more popular the movement became, the more that the destroyer of revivals crept in, which is almost always *the control spirit.*

Bartleman issued a prophetic warning that the grace of God would be lifted if they tried to organize the move of the Holy Spirit. He exhorted them that the Lord had to be free to move and that the true Pentecost could not become a sectarian barrier, but must remain available to all people. "To try to formulate a separate body is but to advertise our failure," he concluded.

The very next day when the people came to the meeting, there was a sign hanging on the building, which read "Apostolic Faith Mission." Bartleman knew then that the beginning of the end had come for that little mission. He was right.

From that time forward, the trouble and division began. Rivalry between the mission and other churches arose. The grace of the Holy Spirit to subdue the presumptuous was lifted, and contention entered the meetings. Strange doctrines started to come forth and bring more reproach. In the beginning, the Spirit's work had been so deep, and the people so hungry for only God, that any time a carnal, human spirit was interjected into the meetings it was discerned as easily as if a stranger had broken into a private group. Now open fanaticism went unchecked. The handwriting was on the wall. The glory had departed.

By the end of 1907, it seemed that a control spirit had taken the place of the Holy Spirit, not just at Azusa but at many of the other Pentecostal meetings in the city as well. There was little discernable love between the brethren as the fights between them became increasingly vicious. This was the final affront to the presence of the Holy Spirit at Azusa, and He departed. The move would go on and ultimately become possibly the greatest move of God in church history, but the mission at Azusa faded into obscurity, and then died altogether.

Today there is a parking lot where the little mission stood. Although the revival's ending was not what was desired, we can be sure that in heaven, there is a monument to the great souls of Azusa Street who wanted God so much, they were willing to press beyond the limits of their time and touch the possibilities of eternity.

Part 2

God Will Do
It Again

CHAPTER EIGHT

THE GATES OF HELL SHALL NOT PREVAIL

According to a well-known proverb, "those who do not know history are doomed to repeat it." Almost all of the great revivals in history died in infamy. Even though Jesus, Himself, affirmed that every time the Lord sows wheat, the enemy will come along and sow tares in the same field, it is obviously not God's will for any revival or movement to end the way most of them do. The enemy has been able to sidetrack almost every move of God by using the same tactics, and still his methods are seldom discerned. Since God desires to use us in a great way, we must, therefore, examine some of the things that went wrong at Azusa Street, not for the purpose of criticizing, but in order to avoid repeating the same mistakes.

One of the most devastating attacks upon the work at Azusa Street came when Charles Parham visited Seymour, his former student, in the fall of 1906. He wanted to see for himself the great work that had so quickly become the talk of Christians around the world. Thrilled by the visit from his mentor, Seymour warmly welcomed and honored him. However, Parham was deeply offended by what he saw. He thought that the various charismatic gifts were too openly demonstrated, and he was appalled by the way so many fell to the ground in apparent trances (one report described Azusa as sometimes resembling "a forest of fallen trees").

While Seymour realized that some were faking the manifestations, he believed that these were tares sent by the devil to foul the field of wheat, and so he held to the biblical wisdom to let the wheat and tares grow up together (Matthew 13:24-30). He knew that if he tried to root out the tares, the wheat would also be uprooted. He responded to Parham that if he stopped that which was not real, he would also quench the Spirit and His work that was genuine. Seymour determined that the risk of having some problems was acceptable in view of the spiritual benefits. He was right. When he later succumbed to the pressure and changed this policy, the revival at the Azusa Street Mission quickly died, and this move of the Holy Spirit was carried on through others.

Even more than the faking of experiences, Parham was appalled by the unusual social and racial integration. Parham admired the Ku Klux Klan and especially objected to racial mixing or mingling during worship and at the altar. However, he did not believe this out of racial pride, but because of a false doctrine. He believed the great sin of humanity that caused the judgment of the flood was racial mixing and that Noah was chosen to survive because of his pedigree, being "without mixed blood." This tragic misunderstanding of Scripture has been the twisted theological basis upon which many racist groups—including the Nazis—have been built.

The Bible does say that Noah was chosen because **"he was perfect in his generations" (Genesis 6:9 KJV)**, or literally, "perfect in his genealogy," but this had nothing to do with the mixing of human races. The mixture that so offended the Lord was the mixture of the fallen angels with men which had produced the superhuman **"nephilim" (Genesis 6:4).** This was a race that the Lord did not create and which threatened the destruction of men and women whom He did create, men and women whom He also planned to redeem. This seems to have been Satan's attempt to pre-empt the "new creation" man that would be brought forth when the Lord gave His Spirit to His children.

In contrast to Parham's philosophy, Seymour felt that an essential element of Christianity itself was a unity which saw beyond the barriers of race, color, gender, nation, class or status. This was a demonstration that God is no respecter of persons and that all believers are truly one in Christ. To him, the Azusa Street Mission was becoming a taste of what true Christianity was meant to be, just as the first Pentecost saw the coming together of Jews from every nation.

Seymour's leadership of a renewal marked by such interracial equality, harmony and unity is even more remarkable when it is understood that this took place during the most severely segregated time in American history. The revival also was composed primarily of the two most embittered racial groups—the poor whites and poor blacks. When the movement spread, it was most readily received in the Southern states where this conflict was then most prevalent. This is a sign of true revival. Just as water always flows to the lowest place, the waters of God always flow to the lowest points, and He sends His light to the darkest places.

Concerning the Azusa Street Revival a leading British clergyman, A.A. Boddy, wrote, "One of the most remarkable things [about the revival] was that preachers of the southern states were willing and eager to go over to those Negro people in Los Angeles and have fellowship with them." Frank Bartleman wrote, "The color line was washed away in the blood."

Charles Parham had been mightily used by God, but the seeds of deception from some of his doctrines were maturing at a time when the enemy could make the greatest use of them. This has been a tragic way in which history has continually repeated itself. Those who begin a movement will almost always persecute those who seek to take it further, or who are used to start a subsequent movement. One of the worst curses placed upon the Israelites for their apostasy was that they would eat their own children. The apostasy of the church has brought this terrible curse upon herself in almost every generation. Tragically, spiritual fathers seem inevitably to attempt to devour their own spiritual children.

When Parham could not force his style of leadership upon the Azusa Street Mission, he denounced it and started another rival mission at the fashionable Women's Christian Temperance Union Building. This was the first schism in the Pentecostal Movement. When this rival mission failed, he spent the rest of his life denouncing Seymour and the Azusa Street Revival. By this, he sealed the doom of his own ministry. He continually lost influence and followers until his death in 1929.

In this sad part of the story, we can see how the enemy will often use spiritual fathers and leaders who become "old wineskins"—rigid and inflexible—to assault a new movement. This is one of the most evil weapons of the enemy, whose guise is as the accuser of the brethren (Revelation 12:10). One of the greatest strengths of the Azusa Street Revival was its racial and national diversity, so this is what Satan used his biggest weapon to attack. Regretfully, we can still expect Satan's heaviest attacks against new movements to come through spiritual fathers or grandfathers who lose their control over the newer emerging movements. Such assaults will usually be directed at what are, in fact, the strongest aspects of the new movements.

The Pentecostal/Charismatic Movement began under the leadership of a black man with a small group of black people. They freely shared what they had been given, and were delighted when they saw the Spirit poured out on those from other races, including whites. They felt that the Lord had given them the greatest gift, and they were thrilled to share it with their white brethren. That this great worldwide revival was a contribution from the black community has never been denied by white Pentecostals, but it is often forgotten.

Many of the white leaders who themselves went to Azusa Street to receive the baptism in the Holy Spirit, remarkably still held to the prevalent segregationist beliefs of the times. They took the blessing back home to their all-white congregations in which no blacks were welcome. This was not true of all white churches, but it was true of most, and the entire Pentecostal Movement quickly separated into the white and black streams that still prevail today. However, this movement did not begin with separate black and white streams and this obviously was not the way that the Lord intended it to be.

PERSECUTION

The spiritual battle that began to rage against the baptism in the Holy Spirit was probably the most fierce persecution that Christians had experienced at the hands of other Christians in centuries. Until the Charismatic Renewal made speaking in tongues almost fashionable, the price for being a Pentecostal was very high. Caricatures of Pentecostals depicting them as anything from devil worshipers to lunatics were carried in newspapers across the country. Employment was difficult, if not impossible, for anyone found to be Pentecostal. Houses and churches of Pentecostals were often burned, and their children were ostracized and subjected to ruthless beatings by other children. Many had to flee from the homes and towns in which they had grown up.

Both the press and historians have turned a blind eye to this persecution against Pentecostals. It was, at times, as terrible and degrading as what African-Americans suffered under segregation. For black Pentecostals, it was double jeopardy, as they were secluded from the white culture because of their race *and* from the black culture because of their religion.

Just as the first Reformers risked all they had so that later generations could enjoy religious freedom, two generations of Pentecostals paid the price for our freedom to know the Holy Spirit in the way that we do today. They did this because they loved the Holy Spirit and counted knowing Him and allowing Him freedom in the church as more important than any freedom that the world could give them. Those who paid this great price for our freedom should be counted as great heroes of the faith whose sacrifices made possible the truth and spiritual liberty that we have today.

Because of the intense persecution against Pentecostals, to add an additional battle with the powerful forces of segregation and bigotry understandably was more than many felt they could handle at the time. Military history teaches that to try to fight a two-front war will almost always result in defeat, so the battle against racism in the church would have to wait for another generation.

Even so, the Pentecostal Movement began with those from every race, creed and social position, seeking the Lord together in unity. The power that was released to impact the world has never been as great as it was in those first years at Azusa when this unity existed. It is apparent that the Pentecostal/Charismatic movement—and indeed the church—will never come into her full potential until this unity is permanent.

From the first day of Pentecost, the Holy Spirit has proven that He will only reveal Himself to the degree that we have unity. Like those who came to the Azusa Street Mission, we must want the Holy Spirit more than we want to hold onto our differences. Christianity was born as a multi-cultural entity on the day of Pentecost when Jews had gathered from "every nation." In the little group at Antioch which sent out the first missionaries to the Gentiles, there were representatives from different races and social positions. It is fitting that in this same way, the Holy Spirit came again at Azusa.

When the Lord wants to do something truly great in the earth, this seems to be a requirement. In its purest form, the church will always be multi-cultural. This is why Paul resolutely confronted Peter concerning his hypocrisy of not eating with the Gentiles. Racial equality before God is fundamental to the gospel: even Peter **"stood condemned"** if he fell to the basic deception that tries to divide both the church and humanity (Galatians 2:11).

It is debatable whether this multiracial nature of the church was lost by the church because of her drift into apostasy, or whether the loss caused that drift. Regardless, racial unity is the true state of the church born on the day of Pentecost when the Holy Spirit first came, and it was this same condition that gave birth to the modern Pentecostal Revival. We will only be the true church to the degree that we recover our multi-cultural roots. An understanding of this reality is being received by many church leaders today, and overcoming racism is now a major thrust almost across the spectrum of Christianity. This is certainly one of the most positive signs of our times.

The Lord is the Blessed Creator who so loves diversity that He made every snowflake, every leaf on every tree, and every one of us, different. Amidst all of this variety, one of the great marvels is the harmony and balance found throughout the earth. Every species of every plant and animal has a part to play in sustaining the whole of creation. The same is true of man. God made man in His image and gave different aspects of His nature as gifts to different races and cultures. We all need one another in order to be the complete reflection of Him. This is why His house must be **"a house of prayer for all nations" (Isaiah 56:7 NIV).** The word often translated "nations" in the New Testament is the Greek word *ethnos*, from which we derive our English word "ethnic." The Lord's house must include *all* ethnic groups. As the church, we will never become whom God has created us to be until this is a reality.

CHAPTER NINE

WHERE THE SPIRIT IS, THERE IS

LIBERTY

There is another great aspect to Seymour's remarkable leadership at Azusa Street. This was his ability to discern and trust the Holy Spirit's leadership and give Him the freedom that He requires. In spite of almost constant pressure from world-renowned church leaders who came from around the globe to impose what they perceived to be needed order and direction on the young revival, for more than two years Seymour held the course and allowed the Holy Spirit to move in His own mysterious ways. Like Evan Roberts, who was at the same time leading the great Welsh Revival, Seymour's greatest leadership quality was his ability to *follow* the Holy Spirit.

Seymour and Roberts both believed that the Holy Spirit required the freedom to move through whomever He chose, not just the leadership. They both resolved to allow anyone to be used by the Lord. This sometimes brought embarrassment when immature believers took advantage of this liberty, but more often it allowed the Holy Spirit to do marvelous things among them. If we really want the Holy Spirit in our midst, we must allow Him to be the leader. After all, He is *God*.

THE LEADERSHIP CHOICE

Finding the balance between God's sovereignty and the free will of man has been one of the most ancient debates in the church. However, both aspects are true, yet do not conflict with one another. Nor is either of these 50% of the truth. Both are 100% true. God is utterly sovereign, and in His sovereignty, He has delegated authority to men and women that even He, Himself, will not violate.

Without freedom there could be no true worship or true obedience. This is why the Lord placed the Tree of Knowledge of Good and Evil in the Garden. There could be no true obedience if there was not also the freedom to disobey. The Lord is the unquestioned Sovereign of the universe, but when He delegates authority, He will not violate it. Otherwise, we would never be able to rule and reign with Him. To rule requires both authority and responsibility. Therefore, even though He always knows what we need even before we ask Him, He always waits for us to ask.

For this reason, **"where the Spirit of the Lord is, there is liberty" (II Corinthians 3:17).** Liberty is required for true worship or true obedience. He has removed the veil into His presence for all, but we must seek Him. Therefore, we are all as close to God as we want to be. We are also as far from Him as we choose to be. If His manifest presence is not in our midst, it is not because of Him, but because of our own choice. Many who give lip service to wanting the Holy Spirit to lead their meetings are unwilling to give up their own programs and fully trust Him to do this in His own way. Seymour was willing.

This kind of "hands off" leadership style has been a hallmark of most of the world's great revivals. However, even a cursory study of church history reveals that outside of revival, it has seldom, if ever, worked. God simply moves in different ways at different times. In times of true revival, there are usually dramatic and unique demonstrations of His sovereignty, and it is best to just stay out of His way. The rest of the time He seems to delight most in working with and through His children. Even so, our goal should always be to submit our will to

His and always follow His leading. The more we can do this, the more He will usually manifest His wonderful presence.

As Vance Havner once observed, "Revival is like a sale at the department store. It is more dramatic, and gets more press, but the normal business of the store is the day-to-day merchandising of products." Revivals may likewise be more spectacular, but they are not the normal business of the church. Much more has been accomplished for the overall advancement of the gospel through the day-to-day witness and service of faithful saints and local church pastors who daily fight on the front lines of the battle against darkness.

Revivals have sparked great spiritual advances, but they are sustained only by the day-to-day devotion of the saints. This is likewise the story of the Pentecostal/Charismatic Movement. The Azusa Street Revival was spectacular, as were other subsequent revivals and movements, but the real advance has come from a multitude of dedicated, but lesser known, leaders and people. Their progress may have been less dramatic, but over the long term, their faithful persistence has accomplished far more.

The same is true in our personal lives. Spectacular spiritual experiences are wonderful and can propel us to great heights of devotion and worship. Even so, the real strength of every Christian's life will usually be found in the degree of faithfulness to the disciplines of Bible study, prayer, fellowship and day-to-day witnessing.

In times of revival, there is a dynamic, manifest presence of the Holy Spirit that makes deviations apparent to almost everyone, including to those who make them. Therefore, needed corrections are usually automatic. However, when we do not have this dynamic presence of the Lord found in revival, almost every vacuum of leadership will be quickly filled with the immature, the prideful, or the rebellious. The result of this will not be revival, but confusion, or worse.

GODLY STRATEGY

It is very important that we do not "get the cart in front of the horse" in our leadership. Seymour could use the style that he did *because* he had revival. If he had tried to use this "hands off" leadership style with the same number and types of people without the dynamic of revival present, he would have had chaos. This has happened to many who have tried to exhibit revival-type leadership without revival. The key is to be ready to step aside when the presence of the Lord does come.

Our goal should be to have the manifest presence of the Lord in all of our meetings. However, the way to do this is not just to sit back and do nothing until He comes, but to faithfully press on to maturity by seeking to be increasingly sensitive to His leading. Occasionally the Lord will catch us up in a spectacular manifestation of His presence, but usually He leads us to higher ground like a father teaching his child to walk. He will help us to stand, and then back off so that we must walk to Him. As we learn to take a couple of steps, He backs farther away so that we have to walk farther. He is not just playing with us when He removes His manifest presence—He is teaching us to walk in the Spirit and to pursue Him. When we do not feel Him, it is not a time to sit down, but rather is the time to try to take more steps.

The New Testament epistles are basically the apostles' exhortations to leaders who were serving in times that were not dynamic revivals. They did not expect the Spirit to come every day like He did on the day of Pentecost, so they went about doing the day-to-day work of the ministry. However, when He does decide to come in a dramatic way that ignites a revival, it is time to drop what we're doing and ride the wave for as far as it will take us.

Wisdom is knowing when the Lord is telling us to go forth with swords in our hands and take the land, and when He is wanting us to stand and watch His salvation. There are appropriate times for each, and anytime we use the wrong strategy in the wrong place, we will have problems. God's strategy is not one or the other, but both, which requires us to seek Him for every situation.

Seymour was called to lead a revival. For a few years, he exercised the wisdom to remain in prayer and allow the Holy Spirit to do the leading (he actually kept a box over his head during the meetings so that his prayer would not be distracted by all that was going on around him!). However, he allowed himself to be pressured into an increasingly protectionist stature by the fierce persecution raised up against the movement. Gradually more and more control of the meetings was assumed by a few leaders, and soon they were following a program for the meetings. Those who were witnesses said that just as gradually as this happened, the Holy Spirit seemed to depart.

This could be the explanation for how the revival at Azusa Street ended. However, it is also possible that it was simply time to move on, and that the Spirit was withdrawing His presence so that the people would go forth. Just as the sale at a department store would lose its impact if it continued all of the time, it does not seem that the Lord intends for revivals to last forever in their initial form.

Even so, most revivals do seem to end prematurely or in a way that may not have been His intention because of human mistakes. We should learn from these errors, but let us also not fall into the trap of wrongly worshiping revival. Even without revival, we can be as close to the Lord today as anyone ever has been. The issue is not whether to seek revival or not, but to seek His will.

Without question, the Azusa Street Revival was one of the greatest movements in all of church history. It can be argued that it has not yet ended, but has gone on in many different forms and in many different places. It is right for us to give honor to whom honor is due, and William J. Seymour must be considered one of the greatest

Christian leaders of all time. He was a great leader for as long as he maintained the leadership style to which he was called, not taking the initiative, but instead remaining sensitive to the leading of the Holy Spirit.

CHAPTER TEN

THE GREATEST MIRACLE

At the height of the Azusa Street Revival, Seymour prophesied, "We are on the verge of the greatest miracle the world has ever seen." The miracle to which he was referring was the true love and unity between races and creeds which he considered fundamental to Christianity. He did not live to see the completion of his dream, but he fully expected the renewal ultimately to accomplish it. Since the movement still continues in a number of different forms, it is inevitable that his dream will come true. When it does, William J. Seymour must be considered as the one who sowed the seeds for this greatest miracle of all. Possibly more than any other man in church history, he promoted that which alone can bring it to pass—seeking the fulness of the Holy Spirit in our midst.

Above all things, the Holy Spirit has come to testify of Jesus. He alone can truly convict us of our sins and lead us into all truth. When the Holy Spirit does manifest Himself in our midst, we do not see the world in shades of black and white; we only see the glory of the Son of God. He has been given to help us see as God sees. God does not look on the outward appearance, but on the heart (I Samuel 16:7). God does not just see us as we are now, but He sees us through the blood of His Son, and as who we are to become—made in the likeness of Jesus. We must begin to see one another in the same way.

The Apostle Paul said that **"tongues are for a sign" (I Corinthians 14:22),** and this sign was given on the first Day of Pentecost. That day, people from every nation heard the glories of God in their own languages. This was the first time since the Tower of Babel and the scattering of men's languages that this had happened. The sign was that the church would be the antithesis of the Tower of Babel, where people were scattered from one another. In the church, all will be gathered as one.

Even as fractured and divided as it presently may be, the Pentecostal Movement has the destiny and calling to help bring unity to the whole church. The fire still burns in the Pentecostal Movement and will burn until all of the wood, hay and stubble have been consumed and all of the gold, silver and precious stones are purified (I Corinthians 3:12-15). Although various movements may each be fashioned into a different stone, the day is coming when we will all be fashioned together into one crown of glory.

The explosive spread of the movement begun at Azusa continued as long as the Holy Spirit was free to move as He willed and the people remained before Him in unity. When the revival drifted from these basics, the people drifted from the source of their power. Where the Holy Spirit is Lord, there must be liberty, and where He is Lord there will be unity. Before the Lord, we all look the same. The blood of Jesus washes away all color lines.

RETURN TO AZUSA

It is interesting to note that the very name "Azusa" was derived from an Indian word that means "blessed miracle." This was first noted by Father Juan Crespi in 1769, while he was on the Portola Expedition to explore California. At that time, "Azusa" referred to the site of an old Indian village south of present day Los Angeles in the San Gabriel Canyon. There a young Indian girl named Coma Lee prayed and fasted for the healing of her people and was gifted with healing power as she laid hands on the sick. After she prayed for a chief who was wonderfully healed, he named her Azusa to commemorate his miracle of healing.

For many years, Azusa continued her healing ministry while her fame spread all over Southern California. During that time, whenever there was suffering, people said, "Go to Azusa and be healed...go to Azusa." Maybe it is time for us to go to Azusa again and be healed of the many wounds we have inflicted upon one another.

*For this booklet, I borrowed heavily from Frank Bartleman's own account of the revival in his classic work **Another Wave of Revival,** now published by Whitaker House Publishers. This book contains many important insights on the nature of revival and can be found in most Christian bookstores.*